POPULAR SONGS
HAL LEONARD
STUDENT PIANO LIBRARY

Broadway Favorites

Arranged by Phillip Keveren

ISBN 978-1-5400-3097-9

HAL•LEONARD®

Visit Hal Leonard Online at
www.halleonard.com

Contact us:
Hal Leonard
7777 West Bluemound Road
Milwaukee, WI 53213
Email: info@halleonard.com

In Europe, contact:
Hal Leonard Europe Limited
42 Wigmore Street
Marylebone, London, W1U 2RN
Email: info@halleonardeurope.com

In Australia, contact:
Hal Leonard Australia Pty. Ltd.
4 Lentara Court
Cheltenham, Victoria, 3192 Australia
Email: info@halleonard.com.au

From the Arranger

Songs written for the Broadway stage have been and continue to be a reliable source of wonderful music for the pianist. Great tunes and snappy rhythms are never out of fashion! This collection features selections from some of the biggest shows in recent years.

I would recommend listening to the original cast recording of each song before diving into the piano setting. It will help you see the "big picture," allowing you to more accurately capture the spirit of the composition in your interpretation.

Have fun with these great songs!

Phillip Keveren

Phillip Keveren, a multi-talented keyboard artist and composer, has composed original works in a variety of genres from piano solo to symphonic orchestra. Mr. Keveren gives frequent concerts and workshops for teachers and their students in the United States, Canada, Europe, and Asia. He holds a B.M. in composition from California State University Northridge and a M.M. in composition from the University of Southern California.

CONTENTS

Falling Slowly
from the Motion Picture ONCE

Words and Music by Glen Hansard
and Marketa Irglova
Arranged by Phillip Keveren

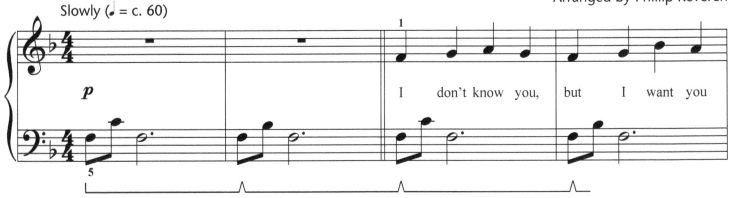

I don't know you, but I want you

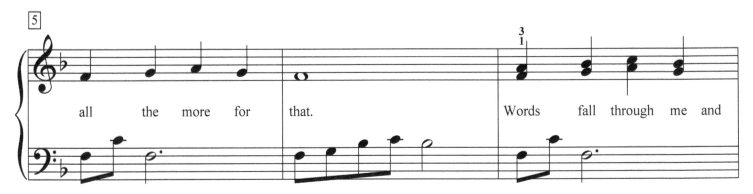

all the more for that. Words fall through me and

al - ways fool me, and I can't re - act.

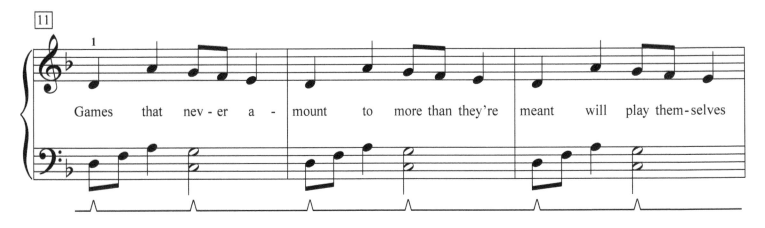

Games that nev - er a - mount to more than they're meant will play them - selves

4

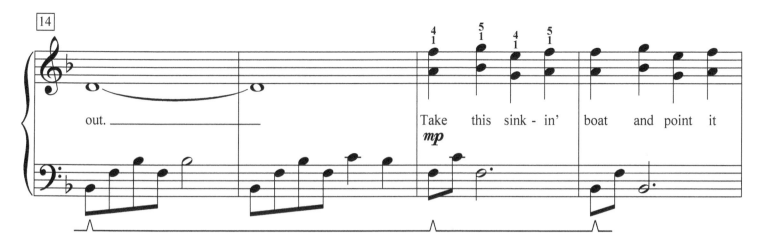

out. _____ Take this sink - in' boat and point it

home; we've still got time. _____ Raise your hope - ful voice; you have a

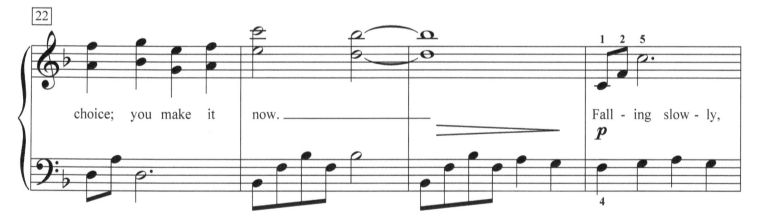

choice; you make it now. _____ Fall - ing slow - ly,

eyes that know me, and I can't go back. _____ And

moods that take me and e-rase me, and I'm paint-ed black. Well,

you have suf-fered e - nough and warred with your - self; it's time that you

won. Take this sink-in'

boat and point it home; we've still got time. _____

Raise your hope - ful voice; you have a choice; you've made it now. _____

Fall - in' slow - ly, sing your mel - o - dy; I'll sing it loud. _____

_____ Take it all. _____ I paid the cost too late, _____

_____ now you're gone. _____
rit.

Once Upon a December

from the Broadway Musical ANASTASIA

Words and Music by Lynn Ahrens
and Stephen Flaherty
Arranged by Phillip Keveren

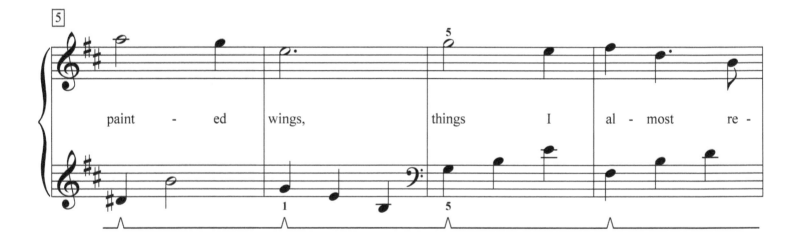

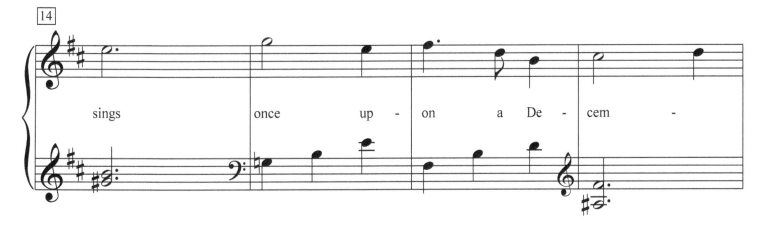

sings   once   up - on a De - cem -

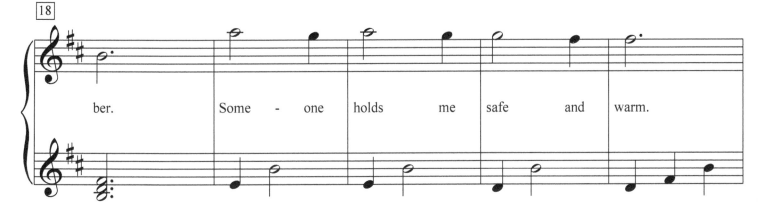

ber.   Some - one holds me safe and warm.

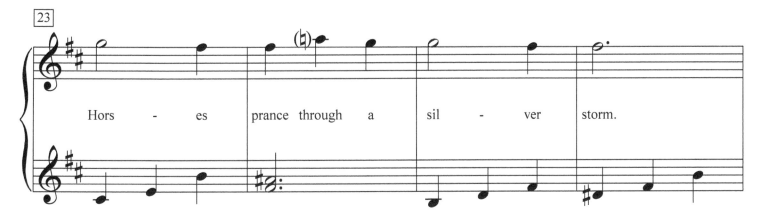

Hors - es prance through a sil - ver storm.

Fig - ures danc - ing grace - ful - ly a - cross my

rit.

9

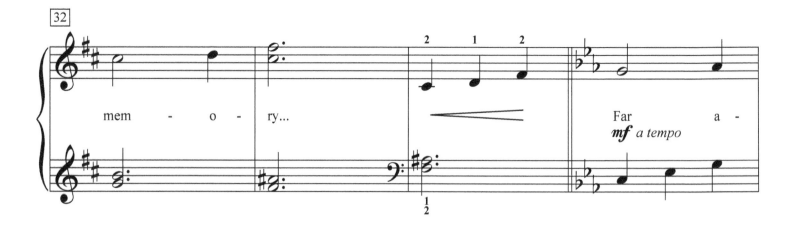

mem - o - ry...

Far a -

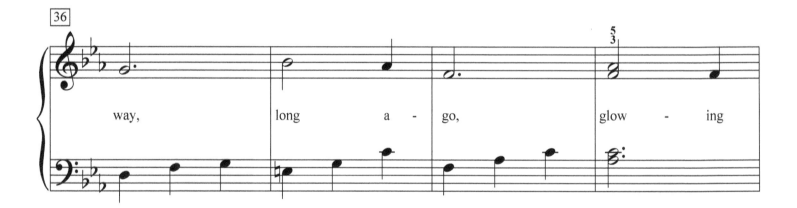

way, long a - go, glow - ing

dim as an em - ber, things my

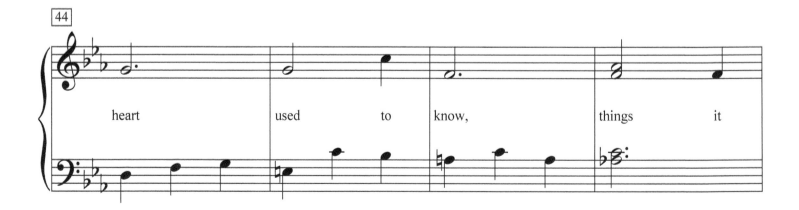

heart used to know, things it

yearns to re-mem - ber... And a

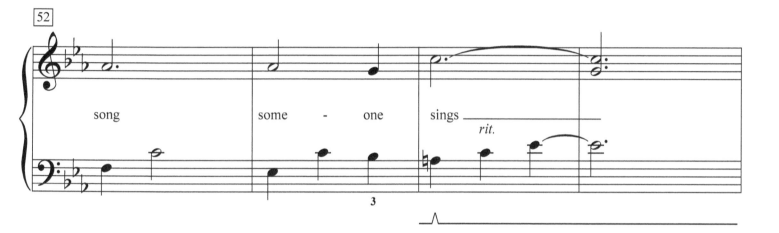

song some - one sings

once up - on a De - cem - ber.

Seize the Day

from NEWSIES THE MUSICAL

Music by Alan Menken
Lyrics by Jack Feldman
Arranged by Phillip Keveren

Gentle Hymn (♩ = c. 84)

mp

Now is the time to

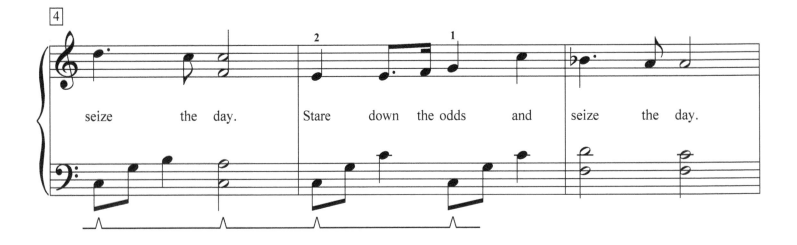

seize the day. Stare down the odds and seize the day.

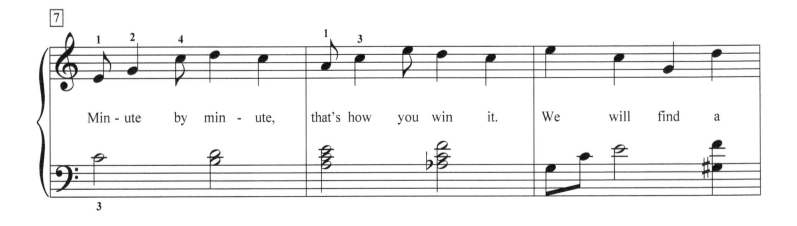

Min - ute by min - ute, that's how you win it. We will find a

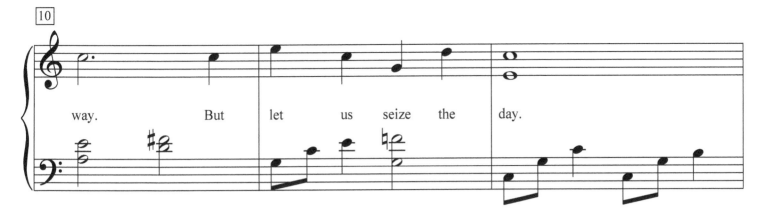

way. But let us seize the day.

Cour-age can-not e - rase our fear.

Cour-age is when we face our fear. Tell those with pow - er,

safe in their tow - er, we will not o - bey!

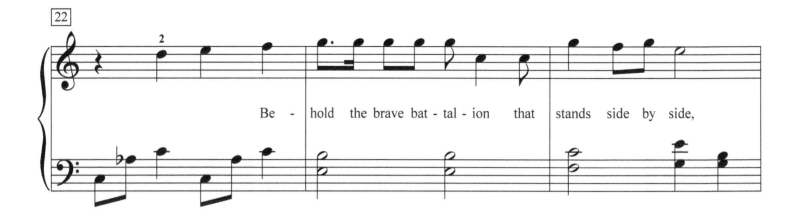

Be - hold the brave bat - tal - ion that stands side by side,

too few in num - ber and too proud to hide. Then say to the oth - ers who

did not fol - low through, "You're still our broth - ers, and
cresc.

we will fight for you." Now is the time to seize the day.
f

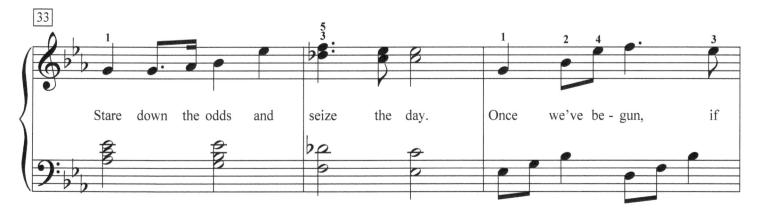

Stare down the odds and seize the day. Once we've be - gun, if

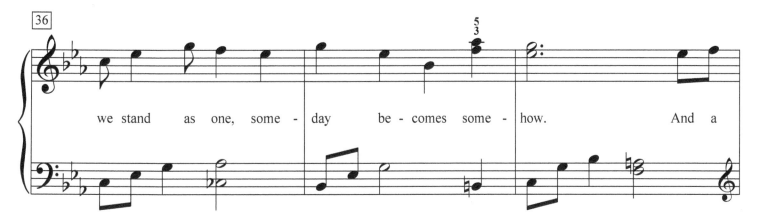

we stand as one, some - day be - comes some - how. And a

prayer be - comes a vow. And the strike starts

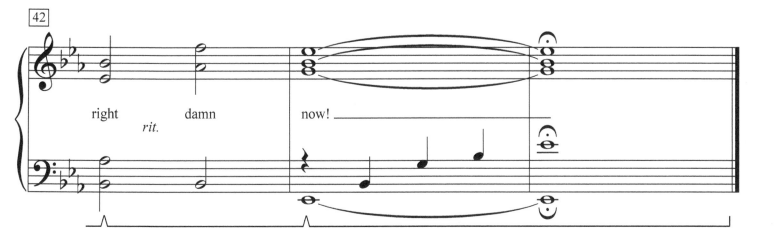

right *rit.* damn now!

She Used to Be Mine

from WAITRESS THE MUSICAL

Words and Music by
Sara Bareilles
Arranged by Phillip Keveren

gave them. _____

It's not eas - y to know; _

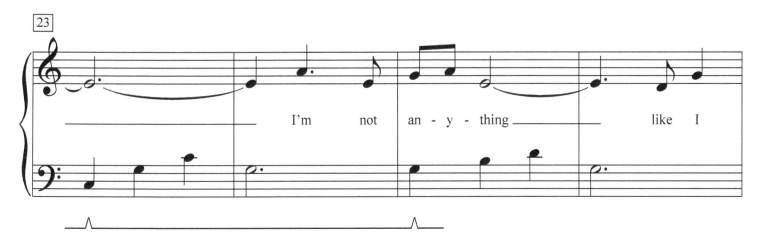

_____ I'm not an - y - thing _____ like I

used to be, _____ al - though it's true _____ I was nev - er at -

ten-tion's sweet cen - ter, _____ I still re - mem - ber that girl. _____

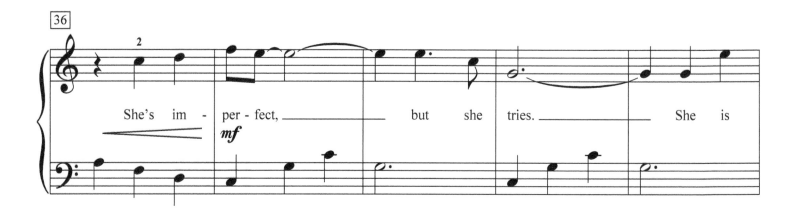

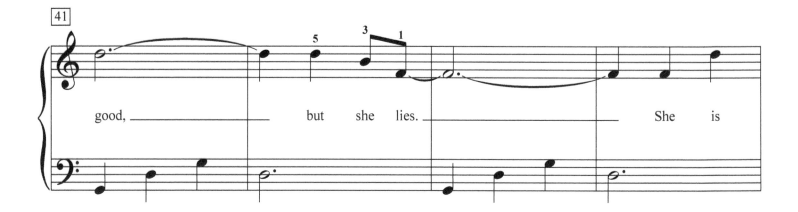

_____ but she's kind. _____ She is lone - ly _____

most of the time. _____ She is all of this, _____ mixed up and

baked in a beau - ti - ful pie. _____ *rit.* *p* She is

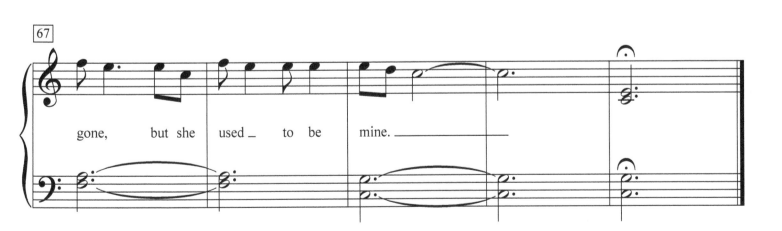

gone, but she used _ to be mine. _____

True Love

from FROZEN: THE BROADWAY MUSICAL

Music and Lyrics by Kristen Anderson-Lopez
and Robert Lopez
Arranged by Phillip Keveren

Gently, with rubato (♩ = c. 100)

p I've sat a-lone in this room be-fore, __ hours and hours on

end. __ I know this de-lu-sion-al wish the door __ would o-pen to __ re-

veal a friend. __ I know this sol-i-tude, I know this kind of cold,

but I had faith in what the sto-ries told __ of true love. __

love, _____ true __ love. _____

mf I was look-ing for a fair-y tale and dove head-first in-to his.

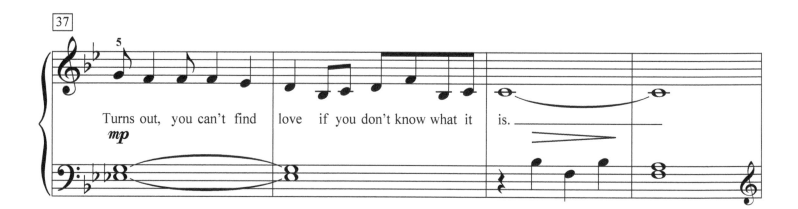

Turns out, you can't find love if you don't know what it is. _____

mp

p And now it's clear I'll nev-er leave this room. __ It ends as it be - gan,

with no one but my - self to blame. __ I played my part __

in the plan. __ Dream-ing got me here, and yet the dream won't die. I

can't wish it a-way, no mat-ter how I try. True __ love, _____ true __

a tempo

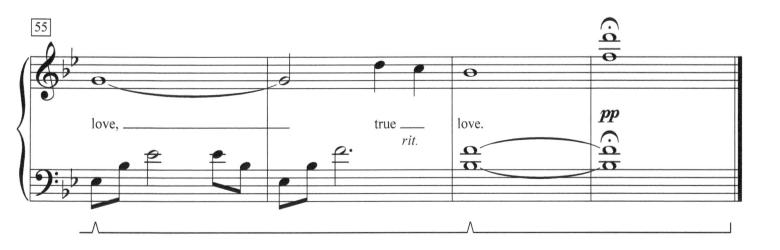

love, _____ true ____ love.

rit.

pp

Waving Through a Window

from DEAR EVAN HANSEN

Music and Lyrics by Benj Pasek
and Justin Paul
Arranged by Phillip Keveren

With drive (♩ = c. 144)

I learned to slam on the brake ___ be - fore I e - ven turn ___

___ the key, ___ be - fore I make the mis - take, ___

be - fore I lead with the worst ___ of me. ___ Give them no rea - son to stare, ___

no slip-pin' up if you slip____ a - way.____

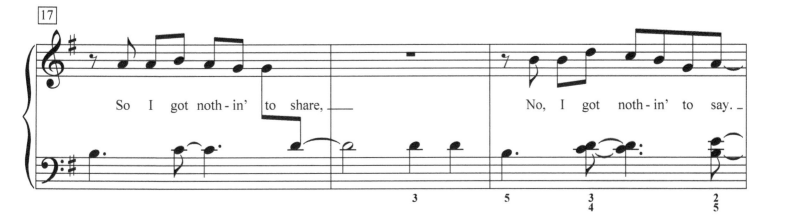

So I got noth-in' to share,____ No, I got noth-in' to say.____

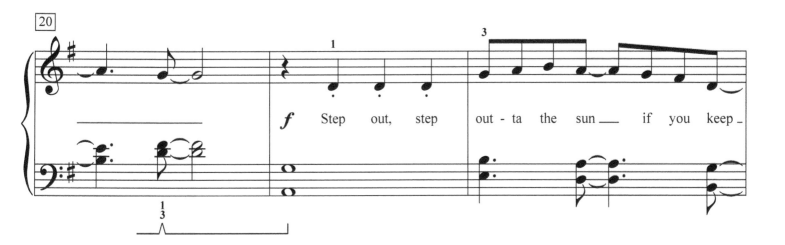

Step out, step out-ta the sun____ if you keep____

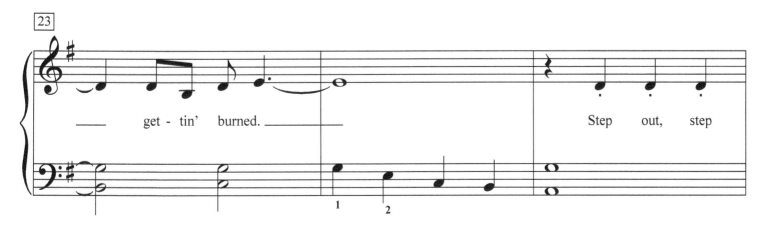

____ get-tin' burned.____ Step out, step

out - ta the sun___ be - cause you've learned,_ be - cause you've learned._

mf On the out - side al - ways look - in' in, will I

ev - er be ___ more than I've al - ways been? 'Cause I'm tap tap tap-pin' on the

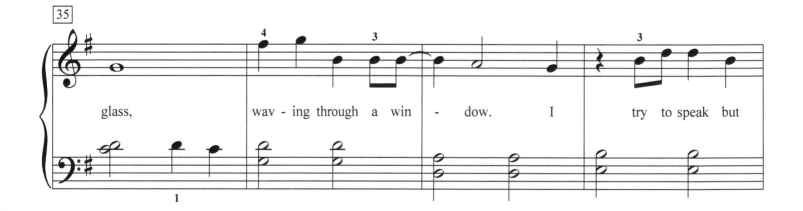

glass, wav - ing through a win - dow. I try to speak but

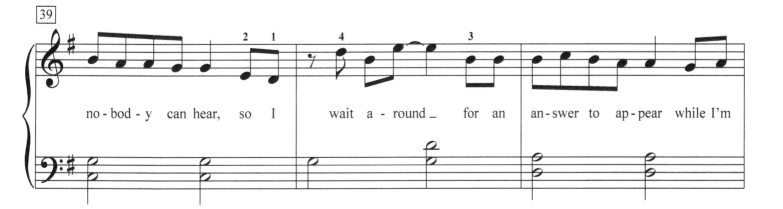

no - bod - y can hear, so I wait a - round __ for an an - swer to ap - pear while I'm

watch watch watch - in' peo - ple pass, wav - ing through a win -

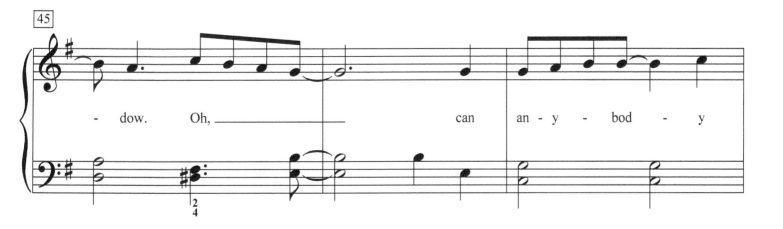

- dow. Oh, _____ can an - y - bod - y

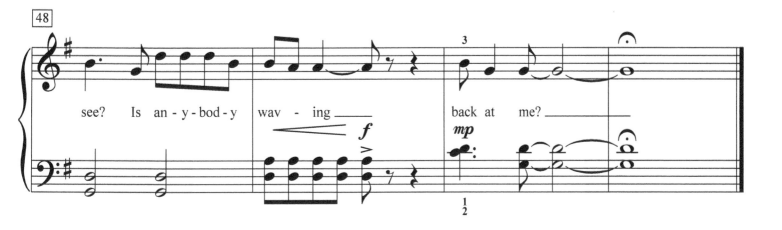

see? Is an - y - bod - y wav - ing __ back at me? __

27

When I Grow Up

from MATILDA THE MUSICAL

Words and Music by
Tim Minchin
Arranged by Phillip Keveren

When I grow up,

I will be tall e - nough to reach the branch - es

that I need to reach to climb the trees you get to

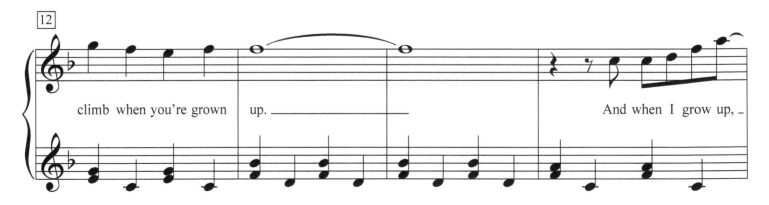

climb when you're grown up. And when I grow up,

I will be smart e - nough __ to an -

- swer all __ the ques - tions that you need __ to know __ the an -

- swers to be - fore you're grown up. __

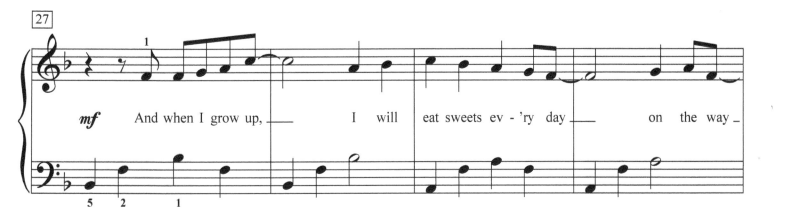

mf And when I grow up, __ I will eat sweets ev - 'ry day __ on the way __

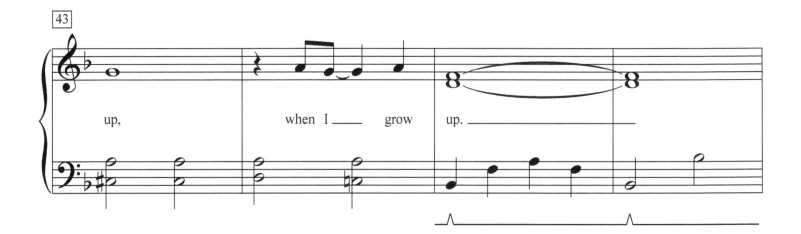

when I grow up, I will be brave e - nough ___ to fight ___

___ the crea - tures that you have ___ to fight ___ be - neath ___ the bed ___

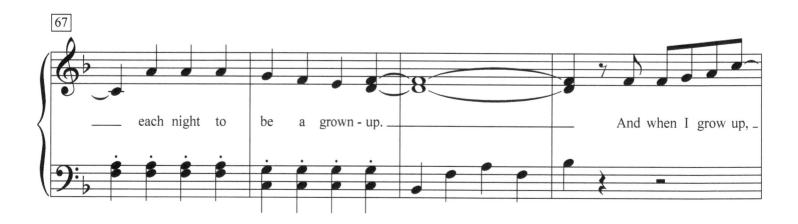

___ each night to be a grown - up. ___ And when I grow up, ___

___ I will have treats ev - 'ry day, ___ and I'll play ___

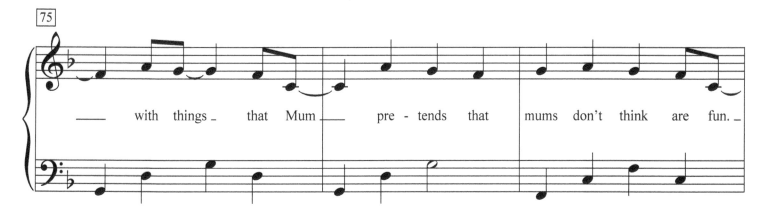

with things ___ that Mum ___ pre - tends that mums don't think are fun. ___

And I will wake up ___ when the sun ___ comes up, and I ___

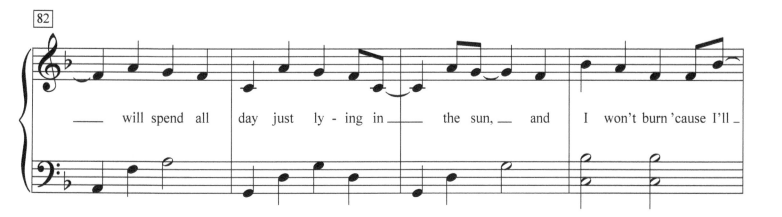

will spend all day just ly - ing in ___ the sun, ___ and I won't burn 'cause I'll ___

be all grown up when I ___ grow up.

mp rit.

You'll Be Back

from HAMILTON

Words and Music by
Lin-Manuel Miranda
Arranged by Phillip Keveren

You say ____ the price of my love's ____ not a price ____ that you're will-ing to pay. ____

____ You cry ____ in your tea ____ which you hurl ____ in the sea ____

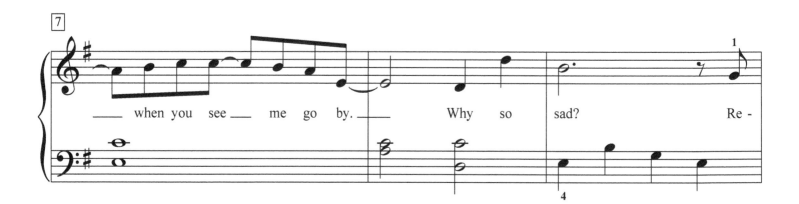

____ when you see ____ me go by. ____ Why so sad? ____ Re-

mem-ber we made ____ an ar-range - ment when you ____ went a - way, ____ now you're mak-ing me

mad. _____ Re - mem - ber, de - spite _ our es - trange - ment, I'm your
rit.

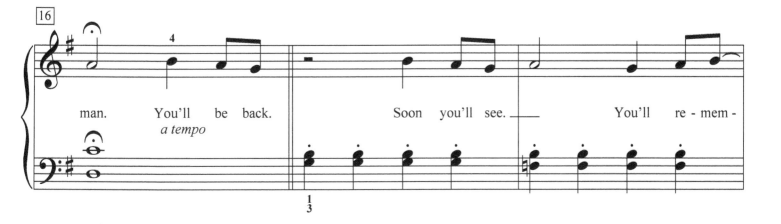

man. You'll be back. Soon you'll see. _ You'll re - mem -
a tempo

- ber you be - long to me. _ You'll be back. Time will tell. _

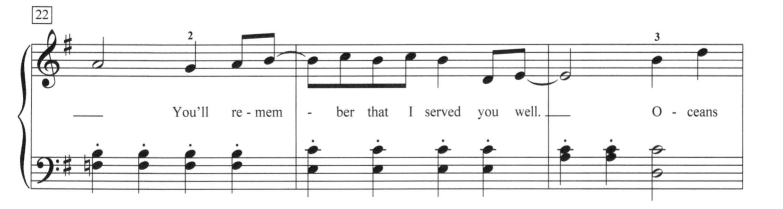

_ You'll re - mem - ber that I served you well. _ O - ceans

rise, em-pires fall, ___ we have seen ___ each oth-er through it all, ___

___ and when push comes to shove, ___ I will send ___

___ a ful-ly armed bat-tal - lion to re-mind you of my love! Da-da-da dat-da, ___

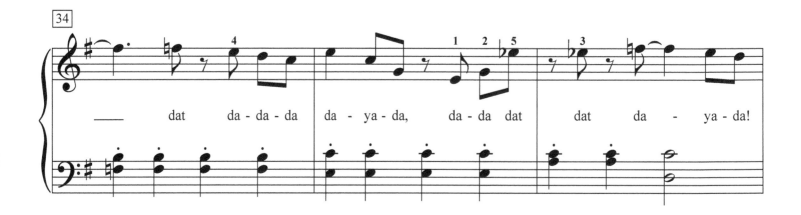

___ dat da-da-da da-ya-da, da-da dat dat da-ya-da!

Da - da - da dat - da, ____ dat da - da - da da - ya - da, da - da dat

dat da. ____ You say ____ our love ____ is drain-ing, and you can't go on. ____

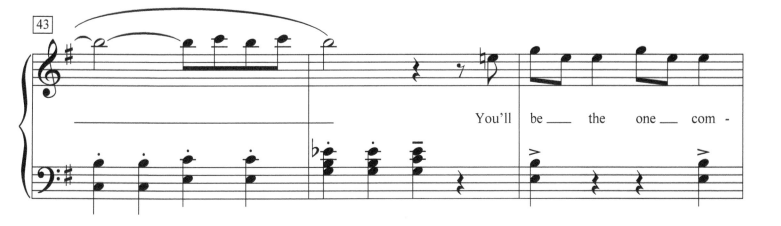

You'll be ____ the one ____ com -

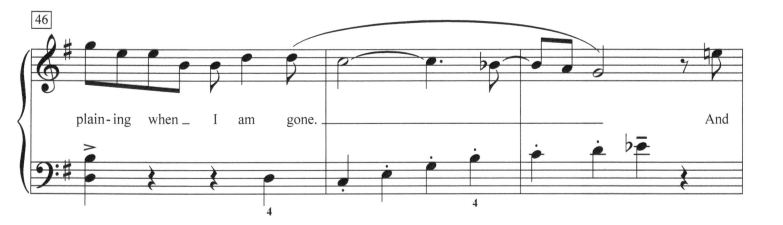

plain-ing when ____ I am gone. ____ And

no, don't change the sub - ject _____ 'cause you're _ my fa - v'rite sub -

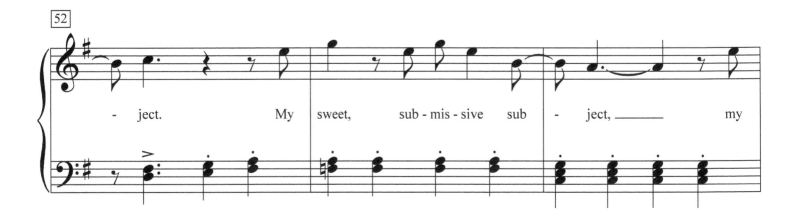

- ject. My sweet, sub - mis - sive sub - ject, _____ my

loy - al roy - al sub - ject, _____ for - ev - er _____ and

ev - er and ev - er and ev - er and ev - er. You'll be back like be - fore. _

I will fight ___ the fight and win the war ___ for your love, _

___ for your praise, ___ and I'll love ___ you to my dy-ing days.

___ When you're gone ___ I'll ___ go mad, ___ so don't throw _

___ a-way this thing we had. ___ 'Cause when push comes to shove, ___ I will kill _

dim. *rit.*